FORTNITE:
Weapons

CHERRY LAKE PUBLISHING • ANN ARBOR, MICHIGAN

by Josh Gregory

Published in the United States of America by Cherry Lake Publishing
Ann Arbor, Michigan
www.cherrylakepublishing.com

Reading Adviser: Marla Conn MS, Ed., Literacy specialist, Read-Ability, Inc.

Library of Congress Cataloging-in-Publication Data
Names: Gregory, Josh, author.
Title: Fortnite. Weapons / by Josh Gregory.
Other titles: Weapons
Description: Ann Arbor, Michigan : Cherry Lake Publishing, 2019. | Series:
    Unofficial guides | Series: 21st century skills innovation library |
    Includes bibliographical references and index. | Audience: Grade 4 to 6.
Identifiers: LCCN 2019003338 | ISBN 9781534148147 [lib. bdg.] |
    ISBN 9781534151000 [pbk.] | ISBN 9781534149571 [pdf] |
    ISBN 9781534152434 [ebook]
Subjects: LCSH: Fortnite [Video game]—Juvenile literature.
Classification: LCC GV1469.35.F67 G748 2019 | DDC 794.8—dc23
LC record available at https://lccn.loc.gov/2019003338

Cherry Lake Publishing would like to acknowledge the work of the Partnership for
21st Century Learning. Please visit www.p21.org for more information.

Printed in the United States of America
Corporate Graphics

21st **Century Skills** INNOVATION LIBRARY

Contents

Chapter 1

Take Aim

Are you one of the hundreds of millions of people around the world who have played *Fortnite*? Or maybe you're thinking of trying it out because all your friends are talking about it. If you're new to

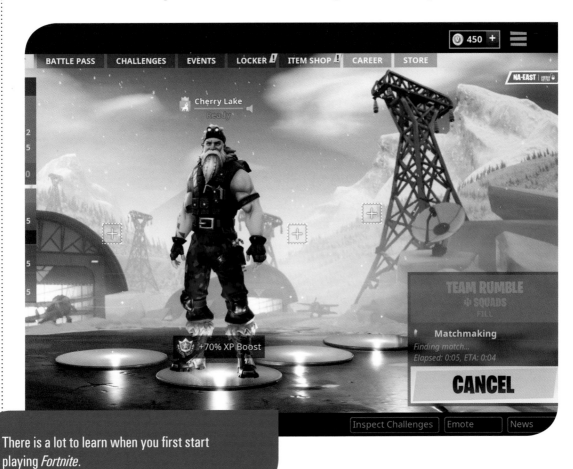

There is a lot to learn when you first start playing *Fortnite*.

Starting each match without any weapons might seem scary, but it is all part of the fun in *Fortnite*.

competitive online battle games, getting started with *Fortnite* can be overwhelming at first. Even if you just want to jump in and join the fight, there is a lot to learn before you can do much of anything.

The first time you dive out of the Battle Bus and land on the *Fortnite* island, you will notice that you don't start out with any weapons! In this game, you have to **scavenge** for the tools you need to win. Of course, this includes weapons. After all, you can't expect to win a fight against a well-armed opponent with your bare hands.

At first, this might seem like no problem. Soon after you land on the island in your first match, you'll start seeing weapons everywhere. Some are lying on the ground. Others are inside treasure chests or packed into the game's famous Supply Llamas. In fact, it probably won't take you long to find more weapons than your character can carry!

You'll find an incredible range of weapons as you play the game.

Once you're fully armed, you may feel like you'll be able to take on anyone you see. But when you take your shiny new weapons into your first fight, you may find that they aren't as effective as you thought they would be. Your enemies seem to do so much more damage than you do. They can hit you from far across the map while tossing grenades at you at the same time. It may seem a little bit unfair. Why are enemy weapons working so much better than yours?

One reason your opponents seem so good is that they have probably practiced a lot. They are highly skilled and have fast reflexes. But they also have a better understanding of how *Fortnite* works. Part of this involves learning what all the different weapons are and how they work. Each weapon has strengths and weaknesses that make it useful in different situations. And some weapons are simply more powerful than others.

This might seem like a lot to learn at first. As you play, you'll notice that *Fortnite* has an incredible variety of weapons to choose from. You'll pick up everything from pistols to rocket launchers. They come in different colors, and some have features that others lack. When you open up your **inventory** screen, you'll notice that each weapon has several **statistics** measuring its abilities. These include DPS, damage, fire rate, **magazine** size, and reload time. DPS stands for damage per second. It tells you how quickly you can damage your enemies if you fire at them as quickly as possible and hit them every time. The statistic labeled "damage," on the other hand, tells you how much damage each shot does. Fire rate indicates

Open your inventory screen to check out the stats for each weapon you pick up.

Personal Preference

This book is full of advice and information about the many different weapons you can use in *Fortnite*. If you follow along with these tips, you should find yourself improving at the game. But if you stumble upon your own strategies, feel free to use them! Everyone's play style is different.

You don't have to play the game the way other people do. You can use the different weapons in the game in any way that you find effective. Want to use a sniper rifle for close combat? Want to use nothing but pistols? Go ahead! These things might make it harder to win. But you should play *Fortnite* in the way that is most fun for you.

the speed at which you can fire the weapon. Magazine size tells you how many shots the weapon holds before it has to be reloaded. Reload time tells you how long it takes to reload the weapon.

Do you really need to memorize all of the statistics for every weapon to be good at *Fortnite*? Of course not! You just need to learn what it all means. Then you will be able to choose exactly the right weapon for each situation. Before long, the game will start to seem a lot easier. Read on to discover the many types of weapons you'll find in *Fortnite*.

Chapter 2

Gear for Every Situation

While there are many different weapons in *Fortnite*, they can all be organized into a few major categories. All of the weapons within each category can be used in pretty much the same

A scoped weapon like a sniper rifle can give you a huge advantage over other players.

Zooming in with non-scoped weapons will still allow you to aim more carefully.

way. For example, all sniper rifles have scopes that allow you to zoom in on distant targets. They can also fire shots that travel a great distance. However, not all of them work exactly the same way. Some do more damage than others. Some are able to be reloaded faster than others. But even with these differences, you can be sure that any sniper rifle will help in a long-distance fight.

This all means that the weapon system in *Fortnite* will seem a lot less complicated once you are

Balancing Act

Like many online games, *Fortnite* is always changing. Its **developers** are always looking for ways to add new things and improve the basic features of the game. Sometimes they do this by adding new weapons to the game or removing old ones. Other times, they change the way different weapons work.

Most of the time, these changes are made as an attempt to improve the **balance** of the game. Perhaps one type of weapon is just too powerful. The developers might make its shots do less damage, or they might increase the time it takes to reload. Or maybe a weapon is so weak that no one wants to use it. The developers might increase its damage.

Sometimes *Fortnite*'s players really like these changes. Other times, the changes draw criticism. The important thing to remember is that the game can change at any time. Don't expect every weapon to work exactly the same way forever!

overall. Their shots spread damage across a wide area, so you do not have to aim as carefully when using them. Each shot is very powerful, and with good aim you can use a shotgun to take out an enemy in just one or two hits. However, all shotguns have small magazines, are slow to fire, and have long reload times.

In some ways, sniper rifles are the opposite of shotguns. They are best for long-distance fights and almost useless up close. Your aim has to be very good to use them successfully. But sniper rifles also have some things in common with shotguns. First, they are very powerful. A single head shot from the Bolt-Action Sniper Rifle or the Heavy Sniper Rifle is enough to knock an enemy out of the match. However, like shotguns, sniper rifles have small magazines and slow fire rates, and take a long time to reload. The Bolt-Action Sniper Rifle, for example, has a magazine size of just one. This means you have to reload after each shot!

Assault rifles are **versatile** weapons that work great at medium range. They are also decent at closer or longer distances if you don't have a better option available. They typically have large magazines, and they can fire very quickly. If you aren't sure which weapons to carry, an assault rifle is almost never a bad choice.

Assault rifles are also the most varied weapon category. Some varieties have unique features. For example, you may find a suppressed assault rifle. This weapon works the same way as a suppressed pistol. You can also find assault rifles with scopes that allow you to zoom in, much like a sniper rifle. One variety even has a **thermal** scope. This makes it easier to spot enemies who are hiding in bushes or other places where it is difficult to notice them with the naked eye.

SMGs have large magazines and high fire rates. Each shot does only a little damage, but these weapons are still very effective if you use them correctly. They are not for pinpoint aiming. They spray shots out across a wide range. This makes them good for close-up fights, much like shotguns.

A grenade launcher really comes in handy for destroying enemy forts.

While there were once several types of machine guns in *Fortnite*, only one variety currently remains in the game. It is called the minigun. This weapon handles much differently than others in the game. It does not have a magazine, so you never need to reload it. When you first press the attack button, the minigun takes a second to start spinning before it launches its first shot. But if you keep holding down the button after that, it will spray shots out at an incredible rate. It can do a ton of damage very quickly. However, it can be tough to hit enemies who are on the move.

Explosive launchers include the Grenade Launcher and Rocket Launcher. These weapons do a huge amount of damage across a wide area. You don't have to hit your enemy straight on to deal damage. You just have to catch them inside the range of an explosion. Launchers are very useful near the end of a match, when a few players are left inside a small circle. Rockets and grenades can quickly destroy opponents' towers, ramps, and walls, leaving your enemies defenseless.

Chapter 3

Picking and Choosing

By now, you should have an idea of how all the different types of weapons work in *Fortnite*. You might even have a few favorites that you're starting to get good with. But there is a lot to consider when choosing which weapons to pick up and

Early in a match, it is good to pick up almost any weapon you can find.

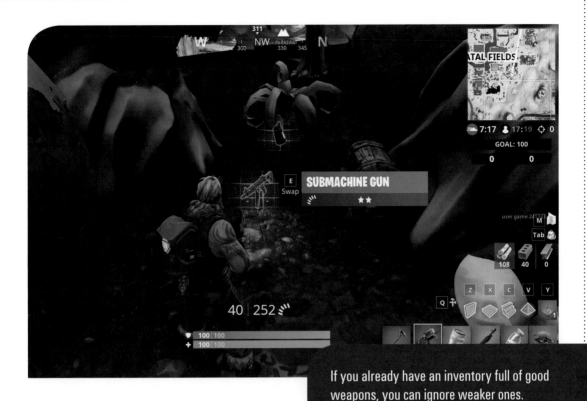

If you already have an inventory full of good weapons, you can ignore weaker ones.

which ones to leave behind as you explore the *Fortnite* island.

The first thing you might notice is that you only have room to carry up to five items at a time. This means you will quickly run out of space if you run around grabbing every weapon you see. It is useful to pick up the first couple of weapons you find in any match, just in case you are attacked. But after that, you should be more selective about which weapons you add to your inventory.

Keep in mind that you also need to make room for any other items you want to carry. These include healing kits, shield potions, and grenades. In most situations, you probably won't want to carry any more than three weapons or so. Try to choose weapons that cover a wide range of situations. For example, carrying a sniper rifle and a shotgun would ensure that you are prepared for both long-range and close-up fights.

This player's inventory has a scoped gun, a shotgun, and healing items. This is a good balance for most situations.

Full Pockets

It doesn't take long to run out of inventory space once you start scavenging for gear in a *Fortnite* match. So what do you do when you're all out of room for new weapons? One thing you can do is open up your inventory screen. This will let you compare the statistics of the weapons you are already carrying. You can also press a button to drop things from this screen. Be careful, though. You won't be able to see what is going on around you when your inventory screen is open. This will leave you **vulnerable** to attacks.

Luckily, there is a faster way to drop items and pick up new ones. First, equip the item you want to drop. Then try to pick up the new item you want. The new item will automatically be equipped. The item you previously had equipped will fall to the ground. Be careful not to drop an item you wanted to keep!

You could then add an assault rifle as your main all-around weapon.

Unless you get very lucky right from the start, you will likely find better and better weapons throughout each match of *Fortnite*. Sometimes it is an easy decision to pick up something new. For example, you might come across a powerful rocket launcher late in the game. This is perfect timing, and it is worth leaving something behind to grab the new weapon. Other times, it might not be so clear. What if you are already carrying a sniper rifle, but you come across a different one? How can you tell if it is better or worse than the one you already have?

The main way to judge a weapon's strength is by its color. Each weapon glows a different color as it lies on the ground. This color shows the weapon's rarity. The rarer a weapon is, the more powerful it is. Here is a chart showing the level of rarity indicated by each color:

COLOR	RARITY
Gray	Common
Green	Uncommon
Blue	Rare
Purple	Epic
Orange/Gold	Legendary

Rarer weapons always do slightly more damage and have slightly shorter reload times than more common versions of the same weapon. This doesn't mean you should always pick up the rarest weapons you find. Just because something is rare does not mean it will help you. For example, an Epic Hand

COMPACT SMG
★★★★★
E Swap

40 | 248

It would be a good idea for this player to replace an Epic SMG with a Legendary SMG.

Cannon is no use if you didn't want a pistol in the first place. But if you are carrying a Rare sniper rifle and you see a Legendary version of the same weapon, be sure to pick it up. It will be a worthwhile upgrade!

Not every weapon is available in every level of rarity. For example, the Heavy Shotgun only comes in Epic and Legendary forms. The regular Pistol only comes in Common, Uncommon, and Rare forms.

You'll also need to keep a close eye on how much ammo you have for each weapon. Each weapon takes a certain kind of ammo. For example, light bullets are used in pistols and SMGs, while shells work only in shotguns. Try to conserve ammo for your best weapons. Don't use up rockets taking potshots at distant players. You can only carry a few at a time, so you

Ammo boxes are one of the best things you can find when you need to stock up on ammunition.

You can check how much of each kind of ammo you are carrying by opening your inventory.

don't want to waste them! Ammo is another good reason to carry more than one type of weapon at all times. If you run out of ammo for your assault rifle, you can switch to your pistol and continue the fight.

Chapter 4

The Wildest Weapons

Aside from the main weapon categories, there are several other ways to deal damage to your opponents in *Fortnite*. Among the most common are handheld explosive devices. For example, you are likely to start finding grenades soon after you begin playing. You can toss these at enemies to create small explosions. Dynamite is another common explosive

When aiming a grenade, you will see a curved line. This shows where the grenade will travel when you throw it.

A well-placed damage trap can be a deadly surprise for your enemies.

item. When you drop it on the ground, a short timer begins ticking. When the timer ends, the dynamite explodes. Stink bombs work a lot like grenades. However, they release a cloud of gas when they explode. This gas cloud will cause damage to any players who touch it.

Explosives are a great way to knock down enemy towers and other structures. With good aim, you can knock out the lower levels of a structure, causing the whole thing to fall down.

You can also damage enemies by adding traps to your own structures. These tricky devices can be placed on floors, walls, and ceilings. When enemy players run past them, they will trigger and cause a lot of damage.

Not all weapons in *Fortnite* can be carried around. If you find a mounted turret, you can attach it to one of your buildings. Approach the turret and press the use button to take control of it. Now you can aim and fire it like a standard weapon. It is very powerful, but you can't move while you fire it. This makes it good for defending a tower, but it does leave you open to attacks if you don't have walls to protect you.

You can do a lot of damage from a mounted turret.

For a Limited Time Only ...

Sometimes you might jump into a new *Fortnite* match and discover a weapon unlike anything you've seen before. On December 10, 2018, players logged in to discover a new item called the Infinity Blade. This powerful sword was found in the same location each match. But just a few days later, on December 14, the Infinity Blade was nowhere to be seen. The *Fortnite* developers had removed it from the game!

The Infinity Blade was only ever meant to be available for a limited time as part of a special event. This was not the only time there was a special limited item in *Fortnite*. Another example was the Infinity Gauntlet, an item that let players briefly transform into Thanos from the *Avengers* movies. These kinds of limited items encourage players to log in often so they don't miss out on the fun.

Try playing with all the different weapon types to get a feel for them. You will probably find that you are better at using some than others. But you never know which weapons you will be lucky enough to find in a match of *Fortnite*. This means you should try to get good with all of them just in case you get stuck using one of your less favorite weapons.

Of course, it will take a long time to become an expert with all of the many weapons in *Fortnite*. And just when you think you've got a handle on everything, the game's developers are sure to add more new weapons to play with. But that's a big part of the fun. Keep playing, keep getting better, and have a great time with your friends at the same time!

Glossary

balance (BAL-uhns) to make a game more fair or fun to play by making adjustments to the rules

developers (dih-VEL-uh-purz) people who make video games or other computer programs

inventory (IN-vuhn-toh-ree) a list of the items your character is carrying

magazine (MAG-uh-zeen) a container that feeds ammunition into a weapon

scavenge (SKAV-uhnj) to search for useful items

statistics (stuh-TIS-tiks) numerical measurements

thermal (THUR-muhl) relating to heat

versatile (VUR-suh-tuhl) useful in many different situations

vulnerable (VUL-nur-uh-buhl) able to be attacked

Find Out More

BOOKS

Cunningham, Kevin. *Video Game Designer*. Ann Arbor, MI:
Cherry Lake Publishing, 2016.

Powell, Marie. *Asking Questions About Video Games*. Ann Arbor,
MI: Cherry Lake Publishing, 2016.

WEBSITES

Epic Games—Fortnite
www.epicgames.com/fortnite/en-US/home
Check out the official *Fortnite* website.

Fortnite Wiki
https://fortnite.gamepedia.com/Fortnite_Wiki
This fan-made website offers up-to-date information on the
latest additions to *Fortnite*.

Index

About the Author

Josh Gregory is the author of more than 125 books for kids. He has written about everything from animals to technology to history. A graduate of the University of Missouri–Columbia, he currently lives in Chicago, Illinois.